Instructional Golf Book

THE R.K. WAY

By Randy Young

**Teaching instructions
on all phases of golf play.**

THE FULL SWING
CHIPPING
SAND PLAY
PUTTING

***Everything you need to know about golf
is explained in this publication***

WITH MANY PICTURED ILLUSTRATIONS.

R.K. means not only Right Knee but also my initials Randy Keith. Power using the lower body with the R.K. method is the only way to get maximum power with direction.

R.K. golf also helps prevent injuries from the golf swing.
Don't be a statistic – it is said that about 70% of golfers develop bad backs, knees, hips, necks, wrists, etc. Some of these injuries caused by the tense golf swing require career-ending surgery.

My Credentials

Great Golf Teacher
6 Club Championships
3 York County Championships
PGA member – 6 years
75 Tournament Champions
Over 500 scores in the 60s
Golf Coach – York College
5 holes in one
2 Double Eagles

Father & Son Golf

*For your interest, this book also highlights Father & Son Golf.
The Topics should help you understand our history and thoughts on golf.*

Order this book online at www.trafford.com/06-1962
or email orders@trafford.com

Most Trafford titles are also available at major online book retailers.

Note for Librarians: A cataloguing record for this book is available from Library and Archives Canada at www.collectionscanada.ca/amicus/index-e.html

ISBN: 978-1-4251-0205-0

We at Trafford believe that it is the responsibility of us all, as both individuals and corporations, to make choices that are environmentally and socially sound. You, in turn, are supporting this responsible conduct each time you purchase a Trafford book, or make use of our publishing services. To find out how you are helping, please visit www.trafford.com/responsiblepublishing.html

Our mission is to efficiently provide the world's finest, most comprehensive book publishing service, enabling every author to experience success. To find out how to publish your book, your way, and have it available worldwide, visit us online at www.trafford.com/10510

www.trafford.com

North America & international
toll-free: 1 888 232 4444 (USA & Canada)
phone: 250 383 6864 • fax: 250 383 6804
email: info@trafford.com

The United Kingdom & Europe
phone: +44 (0)1865 722 113 • local rate: 0845 230 9601
facsimile: +44 (0)1865 722 868 • email: info.uk@trafford.com

10 9 8 7 6 5 4 3

Table of Contents

Important Preface Remark

Take this golf book to the practice range or on the golf course and have readily available information necessary to learn everything you need to know about golf. Why buy a golf video – you can not take it to the range or course.

Chapter 1
The Swing the RK Way

This is the most important chapter in this book and really is the reason for writing this book.

The R.K. (Right Knee) Way is the only way and the easiest way to swing a club and create power with direction. The R.K. Way is the only true everlasting swing. With the R.K. Way you do not have to think of so many mechanics in the swing and therefore the game is much more relaxing and thus more enjoyable. The more relaxed you are and the more enjoyment you have while golfing, the lower your scores will be (strokes will be cut).

The R.K. method is proven by one question – the question is "What is the strongest parts of a person's body – whether man or woman, short or tall, thin or fat?"

The answer – legs, hands & wrists. This is because we are always using these parts in our daily living. Therefore, these parts have the strongest muscles. And the legs, hands and wrists are the main body parts used in the R.K. Way. Therefore the successful result from R.K.

Now for the instructions of the R.K. Way. Although we do not want to get "stuck" with too many thoughts on the mechanics of the golf swing we must present the basic fundamentals of a good golf swing. These fundamentals have to do with the grip and stance.

strong

neutral

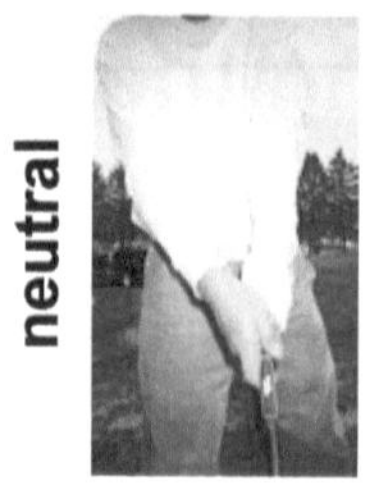

weak

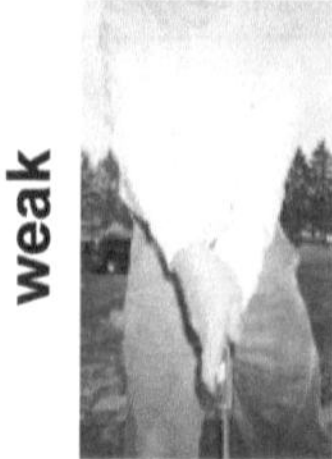

Grip (very important – only contact with club)

Left hand position on club – hold grip in the fingers with little finger anchored under pad of hand palm. Left hand thumb is a little right on shaft. If you can balance the club with using tips of forefinger and thumb your grip is correct.

Right hand position – on club – right hand fits on to left hand – overlap little finger of right hand with forefinger of left hand (96% of golfers use this overlap position). As in the left hand grip the right hand grip is in the fingers. The right hand thumb is a little left on shaft. Again as in the left hand if you can balance the club with using tips of forefinger and thumb your grip is correct. By the way in the overlap position the left thumb is hidden by the right hand.

With the hands in position as outlined above the hands work together and with the grip in the fingers you have better control and feel of the club.

Grip Pressure – very light. A tight grip will create rigidness in the forearms and no body part should be rigid in a successful golf swing. And because the grip is positioned in the fingers more club head speed is created.

P.S. In this grip section, right handed people have a weak left hand. Therefore, they must strengthen the left hand by exercising and also they must definitely wear a glove on the left hand to enhance the grip.

Stance (Another important fundamental in the golf swing)

First consideration – feet should be shoulder width apart.

The stance does vary by person – considering weight (waist size) and height. Normal weight and height with the R.K. method: waist and feet are lined up at least 5 yards left of target. Golfers with average height but larger waist must aim at least 10 yards left of target. These positions allow for the right knee (key to the R.K. Way) and the right side powers to go through the shot.

Another key in stance is to stand tall no matter what your physical makeup. But remember no rigidness in any body part during the swing. In standing tall you should bend the knees sightly. Now our instructions key in on the RK Way to swing a golf club – the only way.

Club position at address.

The hands, arms, and shoulders form a "V" with the butt of the club pointing directly to the belly button – use high hands and don't forget to stand tall. Where the ball is played in relation to the feet depends a lot on the person; also, for longer clubs such as the driver, the ball can be moved toward the left foot and with the shorter clubs (8 or 9 iron) the ball can be moved toward the middle of the feet. As you practice and play you will discover the power slot for you. (or where the club makes the best contact). To measure the distance from the body to the bottom of the golf ball stretch out the "V" to its fullest extent with each club. Keep arms stretched out and very straight, but relaxed, no tension (remember no rigidness in golf). Stretching out the "V" is very important to get proper arc with the club.

"V" formed by shoulders, arms & hands

The butt of the club

The Back Swing (the RK Way)

With the "V" stretched out and the butt of the club pointing to the belly button. The "V" turns back and under and is stretched out to its fullest – the left shoulder is now under the chin. (Do not turn around). This is important – the shoulders, chest and belly button turn back and under and out (not around). Stay on top of the golf ball. This back swing move must be made with a smooth rhythm – not fast or jerky. For a better turn keep "V" and body relaxed. Half way back fully cock both wrists and keep "V" stretched. By fully cocking wrists you will get a longer and smoother back swing. <u>On the back swing the right arm will bend</u> (<u>see picture above</u>) and the left knee will bend slightly toward the right foot without creating any tension. <u>On the back swing, the right leg stays straight and the right foot stays flat on the ground</u>. You can shift weight toward right foot a little to help weight shift. The legs are mainly used for balance on the back swing. The back swing is like a wind up – bending a tree. The more you bend "the tree" the more power is created. In this position and with the wrist fully cocked you are in the firing position. This back swing teaches you how to get full extension and power from the golf swing. You are now ready for the downswing and most important part of the <u>R.K.</u> Way of playing golf. The <u>R.K.</u> Way is the Right Knee Way.

Down Swing

The first move on the down swing – the right knee kicks down toward the ball and at the same time the left hip opens up.

In order for the right knee to properly release down and through, you must push off with the right foot. This raises the right heel off of the ground. This allows the club to be pulled through the swing with maximum club head speed which gains maximum power. These moves with the right knee and left hip lets the right side move through and almost at the same time you start uncocking the wrists through the ball. Your entire body releases correctly when you use the R.K. method with the right knee releasing down and the rapidly uncocking wrists. This gives you solid contact with ball and this gives you the most power you can create in a golf swing and at the same time it gives you better direction and consistency. Please note again that no body part remains rigid – this is especially true of the head.

If you are losing direction keep the left arm straighter throughout the entire swing. The right arm will still bend and you will still swing using the "V." (See pictures in book.)

With the R.K. Way – The Right Knee going down through the shot allows you to take a proper divot. This also makes you automatically shift your weight to the left side. In fact you can walk through a shot if you wish – taking strain off the lower back and still not lose power or accuracy. On the down swing, even when the right knee goes down to the ball, it is important to stand tall, maintaining good posture.

Tempo depends a lot on the make up of the individual – a hyper individual will automatically swing faster than the slower paced golfer. But with the R.K. Way your tempo does not have to change – really this swing creates the proper tempo for you. Good rhythm and tempo comes as a result of the knowledge of the proper swing – the R.K. Way.

With the right knee kick down toward the ball, the opening of the left hip, the wrist release and the stretching of the "V", there is no tension in the golf swing – at no time hold back – release freely. With the R.K. method you will not hurt your back, neck or knees and, therefore, you can continue to play as you age and can play more rounds. And the more you play with this easy and relaxed R.K. Way the more enjoyable it will be for you. You will look forward to playing every day. Also lower scores will be a result. See picture on previous page.

If you want to test your swing, you can make a complete swing in slow motion. You will see how your swing compares to the pictures in this book. With this slow motion swing you will see at impact if your club head is pointed to the target.

We are now showing several illustrations of the golf swing. It is said a picture is worth a thousand words. As you read the R.K. teaching instructions, study the pictures also so that you can better understand this injury-free golfing method.

This page simplifies the full golf swing.

Position #1
"Club at address with 'V' in proper position."

Position #2
"Back swing starts with a one piece take away with 'V' waist high now the wrists start to cock."

Position #3
"Turn the 'V' which means shoulders, arms and hands – NOT lower body. Wrists are fully cocked at top of back swing. This will achieve the full proper back swing."

Position #4
"As your down swing starts, the 'V' will be at this position waist high – the same as position #2. Maintain 'V'"

Power Positions at Impact

These three important things happen at the same time on the down swing and create the perfect impact position:

1) Left hip opens
2) Right knee goes down through to the ball
3) Hands and arms straighten out.

Position #6
"Follow through with the right side and extend the 'V'"

Position #7
"Let the entire right side go through – you will now face the target."

The "V" position referred to in these instructions is outlined in page #6 of this publication.
To practice your swing, do these positions in slow motion and see if you can duplicate them.

Note: On the follow through the "V" stretches out to the target and the butt of the club is still pointing to the belly button.

If you release the entire right side of your body the R.K. way you will end up facing the target.

Now for the short game which is so essential to playing golf. None of us hit every green in regulation – (not even the pros). Therefore our short game comes into play many times on a round of golf. The proper short game – chipping and sand trap play is outlined on the following pages.

Chipping

The R.K. Way is used in chipping. Regular grip with hands – but hands are half way down the grip for better control (remember no tension in hands). Do not grip tight.

Open stance is used – "V" formed by hands, arms, and shoulders again point to the belly button. Still stretch out "V" to measure ball position from body. (This was explained previously in the instruction section of this book.) With the "V" stretched out and the butt of the club pointing to the belly button you are ready for the back swing. Stand tall – feel like you are standing very tall (no tension in the body at this point).

On the back swing for chipping the lower body remains still. The belly button again moves with the "V" as the "V" is stretched out. For chipping the length of the back swing depends on the distance needed to get ball close to pin. Distance needed is measured by looking at the green and pin position from your lie. You should use a club that hits 5 foot on the green. You aim for this spot.

If pin is deep on green use an iron that will hit this 5 foot spot on green to run the golf ball to the hole (for example – maybe a 6 iron). If the pin is short on green or you must go over a sand trap to green and a higher loft shot is required to hit the 5' spot on green use a more lofted club like a wedge, sand wedge, or lob wedge. For a very high shot use the lob wedge and open up the face of the club.

Chipping through the ball the R.K. Way comes into play – the Right Knee kicks down through the ball (don't forget to remain relaxed). In the R.K. Way with the Right Knee kicking down through and the "V" stretched out it will allow you to hit more solid and consistent chips. When properly chipping the R.K. Way you will end up facing the target with your upper body. High or low chip shots can be made the R.K. Way by using a different lofted club – or for low chip shots, with ball in back of stance take a shorter swing and close face of wedge. For very high shots open the face of a lob wedge and take a very long, slow swing. Position of ball at address can be different depending on the individual and the golf ball lie.

Sand Trap Play

Green side bunkers. Again use the stretched out "V" – open stance – hands ahead of ball – now the butt of the club points to the left hip so that club flange digs into sand. Use a firm grip for control when club enters sand. Dig into sand with feet and keep the body still for balance, which is very important in sand trap play. Your eyes are focused 1 ½ inches behind the ball and the club enters the sand 1 ½ inches behind the ball and not at the ball. The face of the sand wedge must be open so that the flange of the club enters the sand and slides under the ball. Break your wrists immediately on the back swing to help dig into the sand make sure you follow through in the sand under the ball. For short sand shots open face of club and proceed as above with a little shorter back swing. For longer sand shots around the green you don't need to open the club face as much and you take a longer back swing.

P.S. To make it easier you can use a 55 degree sand wedge or a 60 degree lob wedge to get different distances – but remember to use the same swing and keep the face of the club open.

Fairway Bunkers (or Waste Bunkers)

Although not a part of the short game we include it with this section on sand trap play.

Again use the R.K. Way – "V" stays same – only difference is a little less Right Knee kick. For a better balance in sand trap dig in slightly with feet. This is because sand is loose and the dig in will keep you from slipping in the sand. Your weight is on the left side and the club is positioned toward the right foot so you can catch the golf ball without taking too much sand back of the ball. Open stance is used and the lower body stays quiet. Open face of club a little bit and aim left. Take an extra club because the above position in a fairway bunker makes a 7 iron like an 8 iron.

Putting

In a round of golf the putter is used more than any other club. And when we putt well the game seems so much easier. We hit the ball better and score well. Putting is very important in the golf game.

The grip is a reverse overlap – the left index finger is over the 3 fingers of the right hand. Grip is in the fingers, and the thumb of both hands are on top of the shaft. Position of the golf ball is inside the left foot.

The “V” with shoulders, arms and hands is still used. The butt of the club again points to the belly button. The tension is light for consistent direction and distance.

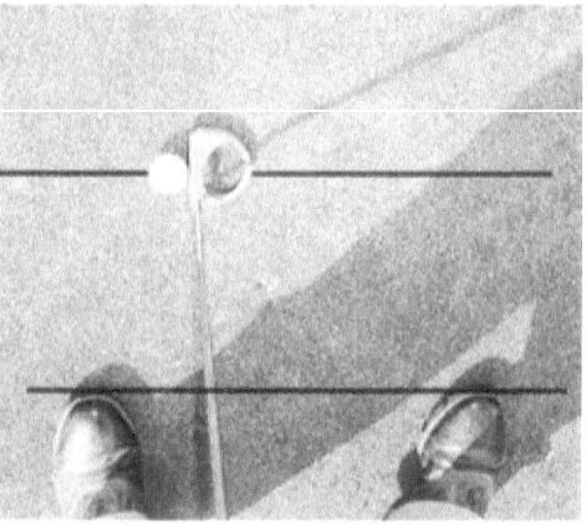

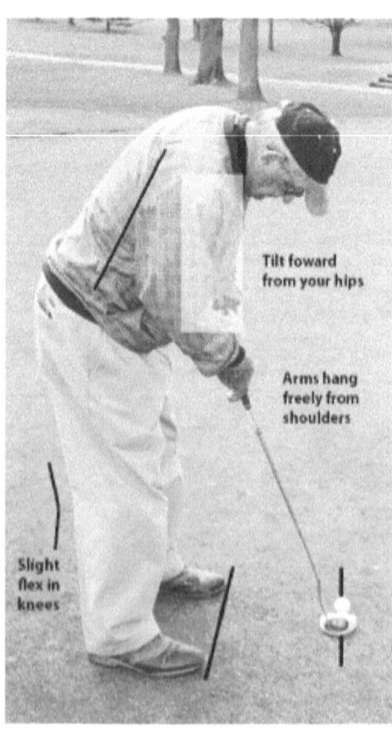

On the putting stroke it is very important that the wrists do not break on the back stroke or forward stroke. This way keeps the putter face blade from opening or closing at any time. An easy way to do this is to keep the bottom of the putter on the ground throughout the stroke – back and through. Hands are straight away from line on back stroke of putt and straight through the line on forward stroke. (Remember – no tension). Using the “V” to take the putter back and forth will help you accomplish this.

With the above instructions you will be able to get the same smooth stroke time after time.

Equipment

We must include a chapter on equipment in this story of playing golf as it is very important and necessary that we have the correct clubs in our bag.

Grips – there are many types of grips available – you should select the one that feels comfortable to you. Remember new grips should be used – maybe once a year depending on your grip tension and the number of rounds you play per year.

Driver Club Head – In recent years many size driver club heads are available. When we first played golf only wooden heads were available. Then a metal insert was used. Now all driver club heads are metal – most made of titanium. The size is important – you should experiment with different size drivers. Remember there is no quick "fix". But today's golfer has the opportunity to hit longer drives and straight drives with the new type drivers. (Remember the R.K. Way is still the only swing – no matter what equipment is used.)

Shaft – This is the most important part of the equipment. At one time there were only steel shafted clubs – now there are graphite shafts with different flexes. The flex you use can vary per golfer. There are even senior shafts made now which should help the older golfer. Our suggestion for proper shaft to use resulting in maximum power and direction is as follows: (until you learn the R.K. way)

Example – 150 yard to the green. If you use an 5 iron now – a regular flex graphite shaft should be used. If you are using an 8 iron now – a steel shaft or stiff graphite shaft should be used. If you need a 3 iron a senior graphite shaft should be used.

P.S. The same example applies for all clubs including the driver.

After you learn the R.K. Way and maximize power and accuracy revert back to the above examples as you gain power and you may have to change shafts.

Putters – There are so many types of putters now in the golf market. We suggest you select the one that feels comfortable to you and you have confidence in. Then stay with that putter – do not continually switch putter styles. If you want you can try a long (belly) putter, but we suggest the regular length putter. P.S. The long belly putter will stop your wrists from breaking down and will help stabilize your putting stroke.

Golf balls – Here again, there are so many makes – with different covers and dimples supplying distance, spin, feel, etc. Use the ball best suited for your swing. Over the years we tried many different golf balls and now use an inexpensive $1.00 each golf ball. We have experienced great results – good distance and proper feel. So many golfers want to use the expensive golf ball – balata covers, etc. The use of expensive golf balls does not necessarily get results.

Chapter 2
Golf – Injury Free the R.K. Way

Learn the R.K. swing techniques found in this publication. Play golf injury-free and for as many years as you wish.

Don't be a statistic – it is said that about 70% of golfers develop bad backs, knees, hips, necks, wrists, etc. Some of these injuries caused by the tense golf swing require career ending surgery.

Proof of the benefits of the R.K. golf method is found in the Young's golfing careers. Combined we have played over 100 years of injury-free golf. Also our accomplishments have been "super." The R.K. way not only protects you from injury but will lower your handicap with straighter and longer shots the easy, smooth way. Our accomplishments (credentials) are listed on the other pages. We list them – not to brag – but to show how the R.K. golf swing can give positive results.

These R.K. golf instructions that deal with injuries and the longevity of ones golf career are the only ones published on this subject.

P.S. Golf is fun, especially with friends and family. Make sure you always keep this thought in mind.

This swing gives you longevity in your golf career and is a golf swing to prevent injury. This publication by the Youngs – Bill and Randy – father and son- explains:

The father, Bill, now 81 years of age has played golf for over 60 years injury-free. And for the last 20 years has golfed every day (weather permitting). He shot his age or better over 340 times. This has been accomplished using the R.K. swing.

The son, Randy, now 54 years of age, has played golf since the age of 10 injury-free. He has developed and perfected the R.K. golf method. Randy was a pro for many years and now is a top golfer in the area. He presently teaches the R.K. golf swing to many golfers who have shown great improvement in their golf game. Bill has been taught this swing the R.K. way and the results are amazing.

BILL'S CREDENTIALS:

York Co. Golf Amateur Assn – Hall of Fame member

York Co. Golf Amateur Assn – Man of Year (1990)

Age shooter – over 250 times

5 Club Championships (2 regular – 3 senior)

York Co. Seniors Champion

Father and Son Tournament Champion

50 Tournament Champions

11 holes in one

As we watch TV golf we hear of back, knee, neck, wrist, hip problems of players such as Arnold Palmer, Jack Nichlaus, Lee Trevino, Tiger Woods, etc. As we play golf with friends (fellow golfers) we hear the same problems – back operations, knee replacements, hip replacements, neck operations, etc. A large percentage (approximately 70%) of golfers experience "golf" injuries to their body. We believe this condition is due to following the "old" techniques: head still, left arm straight, eyes on ball, the reverse "C" which puts tremendous strain on the lower back and spine. These teaching techniques create tension in the swing and stiffness in the body parts involved in the golf swing – back, hips, knees, necks, wrists and hands.

We are presenting here the keys to an injury-free golf swing – for all ages young and old and for men and women. Freedom is the big key to keep in mind. This gives you the proper mental attitude. The R.K. swing technique gives you the perfect swing that will last throughout your golfing career without hurting your back, knees, hips, neck, etc. (The R.K. method is outlined in detail later on in this book.) In the R.K. swing you release everything back and through in a rhythmatic, relaxed, and smooth manner.

The R.K. (Right Knee) method releases the right knee down and through the ball. This right knee release action gets your club down to the ball so you can take a divot and the right knee release automatically shifts your weight to the left side and opens the left hip. At the same time, the right knee releases the wrists and hands simultaneously uncock. (Please note wrists must be cocked on back swing for this to happen.) The wrists and hands go through to the target and this makes the hips and the shoulders open up to the target. The belt buckle or belly button faces the target and also allows your head to go through without effort. This action keeps the spine angle straight and relaxed (not rigid), which is very important in an injury-free golf swing.

The Right Knee release down and through and the uncocked wrists and hands pulls you through to target without any tension taking place. Remember we want no tension or stiffness in our swing. The R.K. way eliminates all tensions. Don't hold back – let it fly. Freedom – freedom – and more freedom. This R.K. swing will also give you distance and accuracy. You do not have to swing hard and get out of balance (fall back) with the R.K. way.

This injury prevention (R.K.) swing has been tried and proven in our golfing careers. At 81 years of age, I (Bill) am still injury free and have experienced no golf injury in over 60 years of playing. I (Randy) am 54 years old and am swinging freely and have experienced no golfing injury – I have played since age 10. The R.K. way is my personal teachings of the golf swing. R.K. means not only Right Knee, but the initials of my name, Randy Keith.

These pictures will show the <u>R.K.</u> theory of injury-free golf.

Chapter 3
Father & Son Thoughts on Golf

This book is unique in its writing style because the authors are father and son. We believe that there is no book like it available. It is about golf as experienced in the lives of a father and son – the Youngs. We trust that the information presented in this publication will be of interest to the average golfer and his or her family members that are affected directly or indirectly by the golfing habits of those involved. Golf can be a plus in the lives of golfers and their family. This book is being published to help make the game of golf a good thing for those involved. Frustration should not be a part of playing this sport and this fact should be kept in mind. Let's have fun and enjoy golf. In this chapter you will read about our thoughts on amateur golf and other topics such as our history, etc.

Please note that this book is presented for easy understanding. It is meant to be short and easily understood (not be long and confusing).

Our Perspectives of Golf

As we journey through playing golf we find that perspectives change as we grow older. Golf becomes more enjoyable and becomes less competitive. Golf is a game and should be played as a game. Winning isn't everything; this is a lesson learned after many years of competitive golf play.

When young, golf is competitive – we practice and practice and we are frustrated if we play poorly or don't win. When we look at golf as a social event and not an athletic one, we can really enjoy playing and sometimes when relaxed we play better. If this lesson could be learned when we are young what a "ball" we could have. Frustration is something that is inevitable in playing golf; swearing, throwing clubs, breaking clubs, and there goes the fun. Most golfers if not all golfers look forward to a round of golf then it ends up as a "sad" occasion full of the "blues" and frustration.

The above comments are not meant to discourage people from playing golf, but meant to help people enjoy golf. We have experienced the different phases of playing golf and thank goodness we now play for fun and really enjoy the fellowship, fresh air, and golf course beauty that surround us. All golf courses have green grass and trees, most have streams and ponds – we must take time to "smell the roses" when we play this great game of golf. Thank goodness golf is an important part of our social lives.

Golf is a helper in relieving the pressures and tensions of life. Occasionally when playing a round of golf, one can forget the problems he or she confronts in life. A normal round of golf can last 4-5 hours – so for this length of time a golfer usually thinks about golf and their game. The golfer thinks about the golf ball lie, the club needed, wind direction, pin position, grass slopes, etc. This definitely helps a person forget about other matters.

I (Bill) am an example of this philosophy. As explained in my golf history as outlined, I experienced many tensions in life. As manager of a local foundry operation my life was engrossed with tension. I dealt with people (workers) from my home town who I knew as neighbors. Also my job caused me to work many hours, but when I had the opportunity to play golf these tensions seemed to leave my thoughts. My wife, Doris, was sick with cancer for many years. I was partially able to cope with this when playing golf. Her death brought on severe strain in my life. Coping with my loss was so difficult and again golf helped. I probably could not have existed without my golf.

Personally I had colon cancer in 1997 and had one operation – then chemo treatment. I wanted to survive because of my family mostly and secondly I wanted to play golf again. My chemo treatments were mild – in fact after one of my treatments I played golf and had a hole in one. Then in late 1999 and early 2000 I developed a benign tumor in my upper back on my spinal cord. I had two back operations. For 5-7 months I was in a wheelchair.

Again after that experience I wanted to survive for my family and to continue to play golf. I worked hard at physical therapy so I could walk again. Golf was partly to blame for my hard work and therapy and my recovery.

Golf can be a plus in life emotionally as well as physically. I know many golfing buddies who have been able to use playing golf as a remedy for life's ups and downs. I present this chapter as a guide for golfers who can experience the same relief from life's tensions and pressures as I have experienced while playing this great game.

ODE TO A GOLF ADDICT

Woe to those – both young and old
With hopes, thoughts and dreams.
All golfers searching for the gold
But only a few succeed it seems.
Because the gold they have in mind:
Trophies, medals, honors of this kind
Are temporary only – and will not last.
Let's play golf for fun and have a blast!

Physical & Mental Requirements of Golf

A person's physical condition is important in playing golf – notice I did not say great golf. Golfers are more concerned about conditioning than ever.

Years ago it was thought that exercise could muscle bound a person and conditioning had no place in golf. Pro Lloyd Mangram was an excellent example of the former – probably the only golfer who strengthened his body muscles and he did play well.

Tiger Woods is the example of today's golfers - exercising and strengthening his body muscles. As golfers we should try to do some exercise to stay in shape. Strong legs and back and hands are a benefit, but not a necessity to enjoying the game. I have seen people play golf with fingers missing on hands, an arm or hand off, even with a leg amputated. These people enjoy the game. And then there is age – personally I am now 81 years old and my golf game is surely not the same as when I was in the 20s to 50s – but I enjoy it more.

Now let's talk mentally. It is stated many times that golf is 90% mental. That is a myth. Golf is very mental – probably about 75%. The mental part of the game is to accept the fact that one day we can shoot 80 – then the next 90. Or in a round of golf we can have a good score on the front nine and then have a poor back nine (or vise versa). One round we seem to make all the putts – then lose it for awhile or one day our drives are down the middle and the next we hit many in the rough. We must accept these conditions without frustrating ourselves if we want to enjoy golf.

These mental factors come into play as we golf, for example:

Fairway or rough ball lies
Sand trap condition
Pin positioning on green
Speed of greens
Slopes and breaks on green
Wind conditions

These conditions keep us thinking as we play and to think properly we can not get upset if we make a bad shot or score badly.

We want to enjoy our golf playing and remember it is a game. We are humans and will make mistakes. (Even the pros make mistakes – but this is a business to them and they should get upset.) We should not get upset. Play golf and have fun. Randy and I have an unwritten rule no club throwing or ball throwing. This is the mental attitude we must let enter into our golf. Why make golf a tough challenge? Make it easy and enjoy it (every round – good or bad).

Other Afterthoughts – Father and Son

The question – how can a golfer shoot his age or better over 340 times and still looking forward to continue to do this at age 81?

Some of the answers are in previous pages – but we put them together here.

1) Stay in shape physically. I began to exercise seriously in the early 30s of my life – using Charles Atlas dynamic tension method. One of these exercises was to do push-ups between chairs and I did this until age 76 (every morning). Then a tumor in my upper spinal cord had to be removed and I could no longer do this exercise. Now at age 81 I go to the gym 3 to 5 times a week for one hour sessions. I work hard to keep my body toned for golf. Also over the years I walked the golf course every day carrying my golf bag.
2) Maintain a good mental attitude. This is rather easy for me as I enjoy the game of golf. I look forward to playing every day and having fellowship with my many golfing friends. I have the ability to play a poor shot and then go on playing without letting the poor shot affect my game. If I play a poor round I want to play again as soon as possible. I do not let this affect my desire to play golf. I try to stay relaxed and sometimes I even sing to help relieve the tension.

3) Over the many years of playing golf I have developed a compact, good tempo, consistent swing. I can repeat my swing time and time again.
4) Talking with Randy about all facets of the golf game has also inspired my play.
5) Recently my son gave me a two-hour lesson in the rain. He taught me the RK way and now I am striking the golf ball more solidly and am shooting my age regularly.
6) During a round of golf together we "root" each other on for many shots. Fellow golfers get tired to hearing "good shot son", "good shot Dad." Of course this is a joke we hear. Son Randy said to Dad, "The best thing you did for me was give me your last name." We are very proud of each other.
7) Learn the etiquette of golf. Be polite – while a person is hitting ball or putting be quiet – don't move. Don't step on line of putt of other players. No throwing clubs. Play in order – low score from previous hold tees off first.
8) Learn the rules of golf – especially the rules that apply to every day play. (Such as out of bounds rules, hitting ball in water hazard rules). Try not to complicate the game by not being fair. Make the game friendly.
9) Beginners should keep score by using method of 5 strokes a hole. For example, 1 over 5's or 1 under 5's. We kept score this way when we first played golf and didn't worry about

shooting pars. It made the game easier and showed improvements made much faster

T.V. and Amateur Golf

It is very obvious that T.V. golf coverage of the pro tournaments has had a tremendous influence on the professional golfers. T.V. coverage has made professional golf a business for the men, ladies and senior pros. The purses are very lucrative and now the top 20 on the PGA Tour will earn over one million dollars. Golfers like Arnold Palmer, Jack Nicklaus, Tiger Woods, etc. have made this happen because their good play has created interest.

The T.V. influence in the golf world has had an effect on our golf also. We golfers love to watch the charges of the likes of Tiger, Jack, Arnie, Annika and now Wie (the 14 year old from Hawaii). And we want to play as well as they do. It looks so easy on T.V. and this has made so many viewers want to play golf.

The golf equipment market has exploded – people are buying clubs, golf bags, balls, gloves, golf clothing, etc. They are playing many rounds of golf per year. This has affected play on golf courses – public and private clubs. Much money is being spent for golf.

Now let's look at the negative effects of T.V. on golf. The costs to participate are very high – buying the equipment, playing in tournaments, spending money at the 19th hole (the bar). Sometimes people cannot afford this, but they sacrifice other things so they can play golf.

Another negative is the time involved. It takes you away from your family many times when you

should be at home with your wife and children. There are many cases when golf causes divorce.
(I have a good friend that was divorced by his wife because of his golfing on weekends continuously.)

T.V. has caused slow play – watching the pros study shots, lining up putts. Golfers copy these pro shot routines and results in rounds of golf requiring 5 to 6 hours. These pre-shot routines really cause problems and frustrations for the average golfer because they do not improve scores that much and the other golfers must wait to play – a round of golf becomes too slow. It is said that a round of golf should take no more than 4 hours – this did happen years ago – but now T.V. has produced more golfers and has slowed down play so much that some of the pleasures of playing golf has been lost.

When you play golf, take the above factors in consideration. Enjoy the game for yourself and others.

Golf Courses

We never played a golf course – private or public – that we did not enjoy the lay out. When playing a round of golf take a moment and as they say "smell the roses". All courses have aesthetic beauty – green fairways, trees, ponds, streams, hills, sand traps, flowers, tee markers and the 18 greens. Another feature of most golf courses – they are away from the busy ways of life – the highways, the noises, the dust and dirt. Golf courses are usually quiet places with clean air.

Also when playing golf we tee it up with other people and are with these people for 4 to 5 hours playing the 18 holes of a golf course. Golfing friends are made which can and usually do last a lifetime. Very seldom have we played golf with a person we did not enjoy. Golf is a fellowship sport – we walk and talk (usually about golf) with playing partners.

Golfing in Pennsylvania – During All Seasons

Years ago most golfers put the clubs away after Labor Day. The golf season in Pennsylvania started in April and ended in September. Nowadays the average golfer plays all year round. (The only exception when snow is on the ground.) This longer season for the avid golfer is possible because of the new equipment and gear now available.

We (the Youngs) are typical examples of golf "nuts" who play in all kinds of weather. When it rains many times we are the only two playing golf at Cool Creek. And as stated before, Randy gave a lesson to Dad Bill for two hours in the pouring rain. We have rain golf gloves (you must make them wet before using to be able to grip the club). We have large golfing umbrellas that completely protect us from the rain. We have rain suits – pants and jackets – waterproof. Our golf shoes are waterproof. We cover our clubs in the golf cart with a large blanket (this is our own idea). We also have a windshield for the front of the cart. Taking the golf cart out with blankets, windshield, towels hanging all over the place – we look stupid, but we stay dry and can play golf.

In the cold, windy weather – November to April – we are also equipped for the elements. We wear fleece underwear and layered clothing (sweater, jacket & windbreaker). A propane heater that fits into one of the cup holders in the cart keeps us cozy and warm during the coldest weather and we also use a cover over our golf cart. We use winter golf gloves. We continue to play all winter unless snow is on the ground. In our area the courses hold winter tour tournaments – you can find a tournament every weekday. We only play one tour, but there are four other ones available.

Pennsylvania weather makes it very interesting to play golf. It is a different game in the windy weather, under cold conditions, and during rainy days. But we make it fun.

Our good golf weather starts in May and ends in October. In these six months we play under normal golfing conditions. But we love playing golf in Pennsylvania throughout the year in all weather. Who wants to live in Florida?

We do!

P.S. An advantage of playing golf in bad weather is that only a few of us are equipped properly and thus not many golfers are on the course. It is like having your own golf course and you can play at your own speed – fast or slow.

A golf cart cover and heater keep any dedicated golfer warm and dry during not-so-desirable weather.

The 19th Hole

No golf writing should end without highlighting the 19th hole. This can be the most important part of a round of golf. It definitely is the most enjoyable. Here a round of golf is replayed over and over with friends. Here we laugh, we discuss, we "needle" each other, we argue – this is golf fellowship at its very best. And please note that although a few beers are downed at the 19th hole, drinking alcohol is not necessary to enjoy golfing friendships. We enjoy golf at the beginning of a round – and further enjoy it if we play well. But when we play poorly, frustration can set in – now the role of the 19th hole – here we return to the pleasures of playing golf through the fellowship of the 19th hole. Those golfers who go home directly after the 18th hole are missing out on fun!

Here's to the 19th hole!

Our Golf History

Father Bill – Born in 1924 and raised in the small town of Wrightsville, a suburb of York, PA. As a young person, golf never entered my mind. There were no nearby golf courses at that time. Baseball, basketball, and shooting pool were some of the sports I participated in. One of my childhood sporting highlights was playing basketball for Wrightsville High School and winning the State Class C District Championship.

My golf career started in 1944 in England while serving in World War II. I was drafted at 18 years of age and spent November 1943 until January 1946 in the ETO. Fortunately most of my time was in England and I was a replacement in the 608th Ordinance Maintenance Battalion. This Battalion consisted of personnel from the John Deere Company who voluntarily entered the war to serve their country. We were stationed in Warminster, England – here we set up factory and waterproofed the equipment for D-Day.

After high school I attended Thompson's Business School in York and learned to type and take shorthand. With this background I was assigned to Headquarters Company and worked for the company adjutant. Here I met Peter Uzelaz, a golf pro from Illinois who was also in headquarters company. He requisitioned golf clubs and we played weekends with the Mess Sgt and supplies officer. Immediately I was hooked on golf.

Then our Battalion was called into Belgium to set up factory and repair tanks and equipment damaged in the Battle of the Bulge. Still in headquarters company and still having the opportunity to play golf on occasion while in Belgium. We played golf on some of the better courses around Brussels.

Golf was still in my veins and when discharged in January of 1946 I used my mustering out pay to purchase a set of clubs at a sporting goods store in York, PA. Now a golf course was present just West of Wrightsville, it was built during the War along Kreutz Creek and named Cool Creek Country Club. Occasionally I played golf at Overlook in Lancaster and Grandview in York, but I wanted to go to college which I did in Collegeville, PA; Ursinus College. Also I met my wife, Doris Leiphart (also a Wrightsville girl) and we fell in love and were married in December 1946.

While in college I played several times on the Ursinus Golf team and during the summer vacation I played with my friends at Cool Creek (friends who were members). After graduation (1950) I returned to my roots in Wrightsville after a few months working in Wilmington, DE. Back home after the war, college, and Wilmington, I was hired by a friend, Don Smith to help him manage his company, Riverside Foundry! He was a member at Cool Creek (then a private club) and soon he paid for my membership there in 1954.

Now 2004 and I am still a member of Cool Creek. Fortunately I was able to play on Friday evenings during the summer. My wife Doris accepted my golf habits and we got along very well. Doris and I had three children; Greg – born in 1949, Randy – born in 1951, and Laurie – born in 1956. Also I joined another private club – Conestoga, in Lancaster County. I played there only on Thursdays and seldom on weekends because I preferred Cool Creek and golfing friends there. I belonged to Conestoga only 4 years. Cool Creek became my golf home.

As I got older and had more seniority at work I would play 3 times during the week in addition to weekends. This resulted in 2 club championships and many wins in various tournaments. Retiring at the age of 60, I played golf every day. During these times my dear wife Doris had breast cancer (lost 2 breasts) and died in March 1985. Golf had seen me through these difficult times (I will explain in a future chapter).

I remarried 2 years later to Marianne Hinkle. I knew Marianne from my high school days and knew her late husband. She also played golf and we enjoyed playing together. I have been fortunate in having both Doris and Marianne tolerating my golf playing.

As stated before I played golf every day as I still do at age 80 today. This has resulted in 3 senior club championships, a county seniors championship and a winner in many golfing events. I have also shot my age over 200 times.

My son Randy, whose golf history follows, played golf with me on many occasions when he was young and now we golf together 3-4 times each week. What a privilege to play golf so much with your son – I am so lucky. My son Greg plays golf and his son, Brian (my grandson) play a few times each year. What enjoyable times. Also, my granddaughter Kristin's husband Drew, who loves golf, plays with us some also.

The credentials resulting from my golf history was shown before. P.S. – my best handicap was 2; now it is a 9 at age 80 (a 9 without practice).

Golf History of Randy Young

Born in October 1951 in the small town of Wrightsville, PA, I was the second of three children in the family of Doris and Bill Young. My brother Greg and my sister Laurie made up a loving and caring family of Doris and Bill Young.

At an early age I was interested in sports due to my father and brother's participation and I played baseball on the local baseball for Boys team and as a pitcher had much success (In fact in one game I struck out 19 batters). I was also very interested in basketball and on a local outdoors basketball court became very proficient at shooting long shots. My grandfather, Frank Young had a regular size pool table in his basement and I shot pool as soon as I could reach the side boards of the table. I have been blessed with great reflexes (eye to muscle).

As I grew older as a teenager in high school I became interested in golf. My father was a member at Cool Creek Country Club in Wrightsville. It was a private club and I spent day after day in the summer playing golf. The pro at Cool Creek, Mike Rooney encouraged me and gave me a few tips and many days I would play 36 or more holes. Without taking one lesson I grooved my own style.

At Eastern York High School, outside of Wrightsville, I continued playing baseball and was presented with the school's Best Baseball Player Award. We won the York County Basketball Championship. I played point guard on that team. These were outstanding times in my high school sports career. They had no golf until my senior year. I played on that team, and was awarded Best Golfer Trophy.

During my high school days, there was a county junior golf program and I played for Cool Creek. My dad helped to organize the Cool Creek team and a gentleman by the name of Jerry Allen transported us to other courses to compete.

After high school I attended York College in York, PA and played golf on the school team. After several years while I was in York College the golf coach left and they made me the student coach and our golf team was very successful. I had the privilege of playing many very good courses; like Hilton Head Island as a member and coach of the golf team.

During the summer vacation from school I played and practiced golf continuously. On one occasion my dad and I traveled to Florida and played golf for a week on very nice courses.

My golf game was now the best at Cool Creek – I had a plus 2 handicap. A friend, Jim Dietz got me a job as assistant pro at the Outdoor Country Club, a private club in York. As an assistant pro, I won the Central PA Assistant Pro Championship. After several years as an assistant pro working mostly from dawn to dusk at a golf course and being allowed to play only once a week, I left for a management position.

According to regulations, I had to wait 2 years before I could compete in amateur tournaments. I could play with fellow golfers which I did at Cool Creek. Also I practiced when I had the opportunity.

During this time I shot many rounds of golf in the 60's. (In my life I shot in the 60's over 500 times.) My handicap continued to fluctuate between +2 and zero. I played in many amateur better ball tournaments with a friend, Doug Barton, and we won most of them. During these years I won 6 Cool Creek Championships and won 2 YCAGA Champion of Champions tournaments. More details of these records are shown before in the credentials shown on cover. Also I tied the course record during this time shooting 64.

After participating in these golfing events for years and having won so many times, I decided that I did it all and began to play for fun again with no pressure to always win. Now I play 3 or 4 times weekly and have a handicap of 5. But now I have found the easy RK Way to play golf. I now teach golf the RK Way and many of my instructions have helped fellow amateur golfers. Now 54 years of age, I want to continue playing golf this way for fun with no pressure 3-4 times weekly and play the R.K. Way.

I want to put a P.S. here – During the winter when it was too cold to play golf, I shot pocket billiards. And thanks to my talent of eye to muscle coordination I won 8 PA pocket billiard championships. I once ran 158 straight balls in a match which is a York County record. I also ran 50 or more balls at least 30 times. At age 16 I also bowled. I averaged 185 per game on lanes that were then tough, not like today's bowling lanes that are finished so to create more spin.

RANDY & BILL
YOUNG

www.ingramcontent.com/pod-product-compliance
Ingram Content Group UK Ltd.
Pitfield, Milton Keynes, MK11 3LW, UK
UKHW041835200726
13854UKWH00003BA/1150